So Many Ways
to Communicate

A new way to explore the animal kingdom

Editorial Director
Caroline Fortin

Executive Editor
Martine Podesto

Research and Documentation
Anne-Marie Brault
Kathleen Wynd

Cover Design
Épicentre

Coordination
Lucie Mc Brearty

Page Setup
Chantal Boyer

Executive Illustrator
Jocelyn Gardner

Illustrations
Rielle Lévesque
Raymond Martin
Claude Thivierge
Danièle Lemay
Nicholas Oroc
Jonathan Jacques
Marie-Andrée Lemieux
(Malem)
Richard Blais (Sketch)

Production Manager
Gaétan Forcillo

Translators
Gwen Schulman
Natasha DeCruz

Copy Editing
Veronica Schami

QUÉBEC AMÉRIQUE

Communicating for survival

Animal communication is all about survival: it's about mating, keeping enemies at bay, protecting territory or making one's presence known. Each animal species has its own language. Some are musicians, others songsters; some roar to be heard, while others communicate through color or odor. Whatever their method, all animals are bearers of important messages. Next time you're out in nature, listen carefully! Every grunt, squeak, melody, shrill cry and drumming sound you hear is part of the world of communication of the creatures around you!

A voice that stands out

Countless plaintive cries emerge from the depths of a dark cave – baby bats calling out for their mothers. Thanks to the distinctiveness of their individual voices, a mother is able to identify her offspring from among the thousands of identical young bats hanging from the roof of this dark den. Bats are equipped with an exceptional communication system and maintain very close social ties all their lives. Like rodents, cetaceans and a number of insects, this winged mammal also communicates through ultrasound. Unfortunately, this facet of their language remains a great mystery…

gray long-eared bat
Plecotus austriacus

Choreography with a message

Honeybees use a unique mode of communication to indicate the location of a new source of food. They dance! By tracing circles along the surface of the nest, they inform other bees that there are flowers close by. If the source of food is more than 100 meters away, the bees dance the figure "8" by vibrating their hindquarters and folded wings. The orientation of the dance even communicates the location of the flowers in relation to the sun!

honeybee
Apis mellifera

garden spider
Araneus diadematus

Soothing vibrations

Like many species of spiders, the male garden spider uses his talents as a guitarist to court his ladylove. To ensure that she does not mistake him for prey, he attaches a thread to the frame of her web and proceeds to pluck it according to a very specific code that she will recognize. After an hour of strumming, she is soothed by the soft vibrations and agrees to mate. But watch out! One false move, and she'll turn her mate into a meal!

3

Fish with "electrifying" appeal

The electric eels swimming South America's streams and small lakes compensate for their poor eyesight with electricity! A white gelatinous mass located in the eel's long tail is made up of muscles containing several tens of thousands of electroplaques that can produce lethal electric shocks. Produced at a lower voltage, however, these pulses send messages to fish of the same species.

South American electric eel
Electrophorus electricus

Are you curious?

Bats use ultrasound to orient themselves. This phenomenon is known as echolocation. When bats are in flight, they emit ultrasonic signals that are reflected back, in the form of echoes, from surrounding objects such as walls, trees and prey. The bats pick up these echoes, which the brain translates into a mental image of their surroundings.

These ones know how to make themselves heard:
songsters

Sound. It travels through the night sky, penetrates deep forest, cuts through turbulent waters. It carries messages at great speed, sometimes to destinations thousands of kilometers away. It should come as no surprise, therefore, that sound is one of the most common modes of communication.

No language is as sweet sounding as the melodies sung by the many songbirds that inhabit our forests, meadows and glades. Unrivalled as the masters of romance, male songbirds nonetheless share their art with several other animals. A veritable symphony animates the ocean depths, brilliantly performed by populations of rorquals, humpback whales and dolphins with wonderfully varied repertoires. Meanwhile, ponds are ringed with frogs of all kinds performing their own tunes.

Nighttime serenade

Indistinguishable in the cacophony of daytime warbling, the male nightingales' song is transformed by night into a remarkable melody that seduces and invites females to mate. Their music, with its rich variations and themes, opens with pure sounds, followed by repeated staccato passages, trills and impressive crescendos – the entire piece punctuated by raucous cries similar to cawing. Hidden in the undergrowth of the forest floor, a nightingale with its drab plumage awaits his sweetheart…

nightingale
Luscinia megarhynchos

Oceanic singers

Whales are some of the most outstanding singers on earth. While the performances of right whales may be less spectacular than those of their cousins the blue whales, their repertoire is fascinating! During mating season, these enormous mammals, measuring up to 18 meters in length, multiply their moos, chirps, whistles and clangs to compose a melody that can be heard kilometers away…

right whale
Eubalaena glacialis

The European tree frog choir

It's mating season for European tree frogs. Gathered close to a marsh, the males join in a deafening chorus that conveys a message… A pocket below the throat, called a "vocal sac," inflates like a balloon, amplifying the sound produced through the vibration of their vocal cords and transmitting it several kilometers away. Each member of the male choir sends a clear message: a song of seduction to females and a warning to male rivals to keep off their territory!

European tree frog
Hyla arborea

The mysterious lyricism of the woodchuck

Who would have thought that this common North American field rodent could whistle like a bird? From the safety of the opening of their den, woodchucks produce a melodious warbling composed of soft trills. Do they sing to assert their rank within their society or to communicate critical information to the 20 or so individuals nestled within the family den? Unfortunately, we have yet to crack the mystery of the woodchuck's song.

woodchuck
Marmota monax

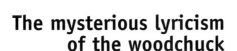

Are you curious?

Birds do not have vocal cords. They sing using their syrinx, a trumpet-shaped organ located in the lower part of the larynx. Using special muscles, the bird deforms its syrinx to produce the notes that make up its musical repertoire.

These ones know how to make themselves heard:
sound technicians

For many, "sound" goes hand-in-hand with "voice." But nothing could be further from the truth! Many animals have developed a very effective language based on simple squeaking, rattling and drumming. Birds produce a resonating sound by pecking at dead branches, fish grind their teeth and the porcupines of Madagascar produce a special clicking sound by vibrating their vertebrae. Discover the fascinating world of these sound effects specialists…

No trespassing!

Palm cockatoos are the only animal known to express themselves using a tool of their own making. They clutch twigs fashioned into specific shapes and lengths between their toes and knock them against the hollow trunk of the tree they have chosen for their offspring. While this is a powerful code for courting a partner, it also sends a clear message to competitors: "Private property. No trespassing!"

palm cockatoo
Probosciger aterrimus

A mysterious ticking sound

These small insects, measuring only four millimeters in length, have a very peculiar way of announcing their presence. Dwelling in old furniture, beams and dead tree trunks, common furniture beetles, sometimes called deathwatch beetles, spend their entire larval stage in wood. As adults, they undertake their search for a companion. Banging their heads and thoraxes against the wall of their galleries, they produce a soft sound, creating vibrations that their fellow creatures can recognize.

common furniture beetle
Anobium punctatum

The big reunion

Every spring, common flickers announce their return from down South. Their unique mode of communication involves hammering dry tree trunks with their strong beaks in a rapid repetitive movement. A flicker's message is quickly deciphered: his partner recognizes the call and hurries to join her faithful companion in the tree hollow they consider their yearly summer home. Once reunited, the love birds reassert their right of ownership by performing a loud tom-tom concert.

common flicker
Colaptes auratus

Drum roll

While the members of a colony of European rabbits peacefully nibble away, their lookout, an old male, attentively keeps watch over the area. At the slightest sign of danger, he energetically drums the ground with his powerful rear feet, then races to his hole at lightning speed! The rabbits get the message quickly: the sight of one of their own bolting home, tail in the air, tells them it's time to take cover!

European rabbit
Oryctolagus cuniculus

Are you
curious?

The palm cockatoos hold several records: they are the largest of the 17 surviving species of cockatoo, and the largest of the Australian parrots. What's more, their beaks measure some 10 centimeters, winning them first prize for the longest beaks in the parrot world!

These ones know how to make themselves heard:
music virtuosos

Some animals produce sound using various parts of their bodies as musical instruments. Wind, string and percussion instrumentalists, the musicians of the animal world form an orchestra that can sometimes be deafening…

Blood-chilling cymbals

Rattlesnakes are highly skilled percussionists! When snakes moult, the scale at the end of the tail is not shed along with the skin, but instead remains attached by a loose cord to the new scale underneath. With every moult, therefore, the "noise-maker" on the end of this reptile's tail lengthens by one segment, up to a maximum of six or eight for those living in the wild. When rattlesnakes are disturbed, they vibrate their miniature cymbals producing a blood-chilling rattling sound. It doesn't take long for the unfortunate soul who crosses paths with this venomous viper to heed the warning and flee!

eastern diamondback rattlesnake
Crotalus adamanteus

8

Grasshopper violinists

To attract females and keep intrusive males at bay, the melodious grasshopper transforms himself into a veritable violinist! Using a kind of comb located on his rear thigh as a bow, the male grasshopper rubs a protruding vein on his wing to produce a series of sounds called "stridulations." The sound varies depending on the species and the message, so there is no mistaking the identity of the musician nor the content of the message!

bow-winged grasshopper
Chorthippus biguttulus

A very clamorous fish

Oceans are far from silent. Some evenings, the noise emanating from the ocean's depths is so loud it keeps sailors awake! Who makes all that racket? The culprits are gurnards. These rowdy fish produce sound by using special muscles to vibrate their swim bladders. The resulting rumbling sound enables them to communicate among themselves and to gather during mating season.

gray gurnard
Eutrigla gurnadus

A brilliant performer

Neither the male's odor nor his appearance seduce the female mole cricket. Rather it is the evening sounds of his brilliant instrumental performance filling the warm summer air that does the trick! In a hole that he digs specially for the occasion, the male mole cricket prepares to perform his melody. He rubs the finely ridged vein of his right elytron against the rugged underside of his left elytron to produce his unique call, while a spherical chamber inside his habitation resonates the sound to his sweetheart's delight!

mole cricket
Gryllotalpa gryllotalpa

Are you curious?

Some 60 million years ago, the ancestors of today's rattlesnake developed their famous alarm system to avoid being trampled by enormous herds of the forerunner to the bison. Thanks to their incredible adaptation, these reptiles were able to frighten large herbivores, thus ensuring their own safety!

These ones have a crying need to be heard!

Some animals are not content simply warbling or rattling – they scream and shriek their messages to make sure they are heard! In the hubbub of bird colonies, screaming becomes a necessity. The piercing cry of penguin parents is the only way of locating a chick in a sea swarming with thousands of birds! In the dense luxuriant vegetation of the rainforest, green monkeys, orangutans and gibbons shriek with an intensity rarely heard – their voices carrying over many kilometers!

The call of the red howler

Assembled in bands of 20 or more individuals, different troops of howler monkeys in the Amazon forest compete with shrill cries and shrieks in a chorus that can be heard more than three kilometers away! These multiple shrieks, primarily coming from the males, communicate a number of messages: they state the position, size and proximity of the band; help to protect territory from rival males; maintain the cohesion of the group; and warn of possible dangers.

red howler
Alouatta seniculus

The toll of the three-wattled bellbird

This bird is renowned for its extraordinarily powerful cry! Perched on the upper branches of a fruit tree in the South American forest, the call of this noisy 30-centimeter tall bird rings out like a bell for a kilometer in every direction! With their breasts puffed out, three-wattled or "caruncled" bellbirds persistently repeat their ringing message to defend their vast territory against intruders.

three-wattled bellbird
Procnias tricarunculata

A cry in the crowd

In spring, the cliffs overhanging the North Atlantic Ocean serve as headquarters for the annual reunion of tens of thousands of northern gannets who gather to reproduce. The male, faithful to his nest site and companion, makes powerful raucous cries that, despite the racket reigning over the colony, can be heard by his partner, who hastens to guide him to the nest through her own calls.

northern gannet
Sula bassana

The language of troats

Head raised high, neck extended, majestic antlers tilted backwards, the male red deer powerfully calls out, producing a sound known as a "troat." In so doing he challenges and drives back his male rivals, attracts females and keeps them in his herd, over which he is master. Unobtrusive for most of the year, this large 250-kilogram mammal becomes pretty boisterous during mating season, sometimes roaring for several hours nonstop!

red deer
Cervus elaphus

Are you curious?

Howler monkeys do not cope well in captivity. Unlike other primates in zoos, these monkeys do not survive in captivity for very long. The record is only three and a half years.

Others just want to be seen: a carefully choreographed performance

Visual performance occupies an important place in the world of animal communication. Species with good eyesight, such as birds and mammals, are masters of this technique. In carefully choreographed displays and shows, certain animal performances combine gestures and behavior designed to convey a very specific message to the spectator. In the heart of the savannah, herds of gazelle leap in unison. Venturing onto the web spun by his ladylove, a male spider makes an offering of food. Clutched in each other's pincers, two scorpions perform a choreography of love Attention! The show is about to begin!

A show of chivalry

The stage is a small promontory in a wetland. Female ruffs sit front row center. Male ruffs gather in this "arena" or "lek" to put on their annual show before an enchanted audience. Proudly displaying their courtship breastplates, these valiant knights engage in mock battles: they run and dance around each other, come to a halt, collapse to the ground, pick themselves up and repeat the performance, again and again…

ruff
Philomachus pugnax

Aquatic ballet

Birds are not the only masters of courtship displays. Underwater, certain fish put on a show of their own. During laying season, a conversation of carefully choreographed behavior takes place between three-spined stickleback couples. The male conveys his messages to the female in a very specific order: he displays his red belly, performs a "zigzag" dance, nudges her sides and wriggles his body – an invitation for her to start laying her eggs.

three-spined stickleback
Gasterosteus aculeatus

A champion in synchronized swimming

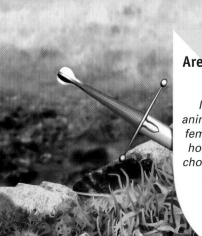

In a pool or a pond, the male newt performs a strange aquatic dance designed to woo the female newt of his choice. Gently prodding her with his muzzle, the newt positions himself perpendicularly to his love and beats his tail from side to side. The speed of this gesture indicates to the female that her courtier is a member of her species!

palmated newt
Triturus helveticus

13

Reflecting mirrors

Pronghorns roaming the rocky deserts and prairies of the American West communicate by means of a large white rump patch. At the first sign of danger, special muscles make the fur bristle creating a huge white patch called a "mirror." This instrument actually reflects light which can be seen up to three kilometers away by members of the herd who receive the message and pass it along.

pronghorn
Antilocapra americana

Are you curious?

In general, throughout the animal world, the male selects his female mate. This is not the case, however, with ruffs. The female chooses her partner based on his performance in the arena.

Others just want to be seen: dazzling visual effects

Crustaceans, insects, certain fish, frogs, turtles, snakes and birds, along with monkeys and some diurnal mammals can see color. Colors speak: they attract, seduce and warn. That's why many animals make color such an important element of their language! While the spectacular courtship plumage of the bird of paradise dazzles with its beauty and attracts females, the white and black fur of certain animals frightens those who have already had the misfortune of coming into contact with a skunk's putrid spray…

The peacock's pride

The male peacock communicates his message by displaying his glorious 200-feather train, creating a magnificent fan of shimmering reflections. Proudly strutting before the female of his choice, or any other animal he wishes to impress (including humans), the superb blue peacock flutters his finery, making his multiple "eyes" quiver and hypnotizing his sweetheart. Seduced, she joins the male's harem of three to four females.

blue peacock
Pavo cristatus

14

Danger: ferocious octopus!

Despite their small size, these 20-centimeter octopuses bear a very powerful message… When threatened, these cephalopods, from the coasts of Australia and Tasmania, instantly sprout a multitude of blue rings all over their bodies. This unequivocal message warns the intruder of an impending deadly sting. In fact, the poison produced by their salivary glands is so potent it can kill small prey in the vicinity.

blue-ringed octopus
Hapalochlaena lunulata

A colorful primate

Although all members of a mandrill troop have colorful faces, it is the dominant males who are adorned with the most vivid colors during the mating season. To avoid conflicts and to ward off endless quarrelling, the leader of the harem exposes his bright-colored face to his adversary's gaze. Convinced of the leader's strength and aggressiveness, the intruder beats a hasty retreat, presenting his posterior in a sign of submission.

mandrill
Papio sphinx

Illuminated communication

These inhabitants of the ocean's dark depths have veritable headlights under their eyes! The light, produced by bacteria and controlled by special skin membranes, transmits important information. Not only does the light reveal the location of each individual in the school, it also provides protection: the zigzagging light beams produced by fleeing firefly fish completely disorient their predators.

firefly fish
Photoblepharon palpebratus

Are you
curious?

Peacocks never turn down a meal! While they prefer seeds, fruit and insects, these birds readily kill and swallow snakes and even mice – whole!

Some let their bodies
do the talking

We've all seen cats arch their backs and bristle their coats in fear. Most of us clearly understand the message being communicated. Like swans who whistle as they suddenly spread their wings or owls who puff up their feathers, cats try to appear more imposing than they actually are in order to scare off their adversaries. Whether it's a show of submission, a sign of playfulness or a warning of attack, whether frightened or excited, animals use gestures and attitudes to communicate. For some, facial expressions and body language are accurate indicators of their next move…

common chimpanzee
Pan troglodytes

Facial expressions worth a thousand words

Chimpanzees will never be able to speak. Their mouths, throats and vocal cords make spoken language impossible. But these primates are extremely intelligent and have a complex repertory of facial expressions that enable them to communicate what they are feeling. These apes grimace when they want to play, smile broadly in reaction to threats, pout to show their interest and purse their lips to convey aggressiveness.

Horses and their body language

At a very early age, horses learn to use certain parts of their bodies to communicate among themselves. To warn the group of their aggressive mood, they open their mouths, curl up their lips, bare their teeth and pull back their ears. Face to face with the leader of the herd, however, horses adopt a very different attitude: as a sign of respect, they bow their heads very low and bend their ears to the sides, sometimes even nibbling on the skin of the leader's croup!

domestic horse
Equus caballus

The language of the leader

Body language is vital to gray wolves. Legs straight, ears pricked and tail raised, the leader of the pack demonstrates his superiority and his high rank within the society. Subordinate wolves show their submission and respect for their leader: ears down and tail between their legs, they approach in a crouching position and lick the leader's muzzle. The facial expressions of wolves can also reveal their state of mind such as benevolence, playfulness, defensiveness and the intention to attack.

17

gray wolf
Canis lupus

Are you curious?

Two species of chimpanzees inhabit tropical Africa. The first, the common chimpanzee, lives in dense forests and the savannah. The second, the bonobo, lives only in Zaire's rain forest and can easily be distinguished by its black face.

While others use odors to communicate

Researchers estimate that there are over 400,000 different odors wafting through the air! With their extraordinary sense of smell, dogs can gather a great deal more information about their environment than through any visual or audio message. Dogs can sniff out another animal's intention to attack, as well as the creature's age, sex and species! The scents produced by animals are called "pheromones," and animals with strong olfaction, such as mammals, reptiles, fish and insects, use large quantities of these hormones. This mysterious olfactory language serves to alert fellow creatures, mark territory, distinguish between individuals from the same species and attract the opposite sex…

A meaningful scent

Muskrats are able to effectively communicate during the mating season partly because of their strong scent… These rodents have glands at the base of their tails that secrete musk, a strong scent used to impregnate their huts and the trees demarcating their territory. During mating, these fragrant messages beckon partners to mate and keep other muskrats away!

muskrat
Ondatra zibethicus

The smell of danger

Many fish have skin cells that carry a special substance that is particularly repulsive! When the skin of these fish is gashed, during an attack for instance, this warning substance is released into the water. The scent causes a wave of panic and fellow creatures flee the site of danger.

African mud fish
Phractolaemus ansorgei

An odoriferous message

Like many animals, hippopotamuses use the scent of their excrement as a means of communication. By wagging his tail from side to side, the leader of the herd spreads his dung to mark his territory in a very fragrant gesture of ownership… At the same time, a subordinate male expresses the ultimate sign of gratitude by defecating on his leader's snout! In less than an hour, the dominant hippopotamus can receive up to a half dozen of these fuming piles as a sign of respect…

hippopotamus
Hippopotamus amphibius

Everything has its odor

Cockroaches, also referred to as "roaches," use the colorful language of individual scents to convey specific messages… A particular scent will attract a fellow cockroach, while another summons a large gathering and a third signals imminent danger… When cockroaches find a source of food, they secrete drops with an irresistible scent around their discovery. Fellow cockroaches pick up the message on their sensitive antennae and rush to take part in the feast!

oriental cockroach
Blatta orientalis

Are you curious?

In the summer, muskrats live in burrows along their favorite river banks. In the fall, they build huts 60 to 120 centimeters high with plant debris and mud. The hut serves as their winter dwelling.

These ones convey
touching messages

Touching is a fundamental mode of communication among many advanced animals. While jellyfish, sponges and certain types of fish never come into physical contact, cuddles, hugs and caresses are a part of daily life for the group of primates to which we belong. Some animals spend most of their day caressing, licking and fussing over each other. This practice, common among rodents and monkeys, is called "grooming." In addition to removing dirt and parasites from each other's fur, this social activity is a very important ritual. It is an excellent way to relax, reduce aggressiveness between individuals and reinforce social ties.

Grooming sessions

Grooming lays at the heart of a primate's day. Some monkeys spend a lot of time meticulously picking out insects, ticks and parasites embedded in each other's fur. Ten percent of a macaque day's is spent grooming. In groups of 30 to 150 individuals, these Japanese mountain monkeys form tightly knit societies in which relations among females are extremely important.

Japanese macaque
Macaca fuscata

Impeccable feathers

Both parrots and crows preen each other's feathers in a calming gesture. Energetically ruffling her vivid plumage, the female macaw pulls in her head, thus gently inviting her partner to groom her feathers. A meter in length, the hyacinth macaw, an inhabitant of Brazil, Bolivia and Paraguay, is the largest of the parrots. As with all parrots, couples are united for life!

hyacinth macaw
Anodorhynchus hyacinthinus

Lobster train

In fall, columns made up of hundreds of American spiny lobsters move along the ocean floor toward warmer southern waters. To maintain the column, lobsters rest their claws and antennae on the backs of the lobsters before them. This single file improves the crustaceans' chances of survival during their journey – united they are less vulnerable to predator attacks and can advance more quickly.

American spiny lobster
Palinurus argus

21

Affectionate rodents

Black-tailed prairie dogs live in small family groups called "coteries." They enjoy regular delousing sessions and are very affectionate in demonstrating their attachment to one another. When two individuals from the same family cross paths, they approach and, bearing their teeth, proceed to sniff each other and gently rub their cheeks and muzzles together. This charming ritual indicates that they recognize each other as members of the same family.

black-tailed prairie dog
Cynomys ludovicianus

Are you curious?

Japanese macaques eat leaves and ripe fruit that they clean before eating. They are the only monkeys to have developed this habit.

While these ones converse
with humans

Through the ages, humans have tried to communicate with animals that possess fascinating vocal capacities or communication skills. There are people who have developed the ability to imitate bird calls and have succeeded in transmitting and receiving messages. Others have taught spoken language to parrots, while a few renowned researchers have successfully taught chimpanzees to communicate with humans through the use of symbols. The most refined and complex mode of communication continues to be human language, however, and while dogs, cats, parrots and chimpanzees are effective communicators, they will never be able to truly communicate with humans…

Long-range birds

Humans have long been impressed by the extraordinary ability of feral pigeons to return to their point of departure following a journey of several thousand kilometers. As early as 3000 BC, the Egyptians used pigeons to send messages to the four corners of Egypt. Several hundred years later, the Greeks used them to announce the winners of the Olympic Games. During the First World War, feral pigeons were used to carry important messages.

feral pigeon
Columba livia

A great talker

Who says parrots don't understand human language? This gray parrot, also known as an African gray, is one of the most articulate "orators." In recent experiments, a young parrot from this species learned to name some 20 objects, five colors and a few shapes... all this in just a few months! Apparently, by the age of two, he even knew how to say "no" as a sign of refusal...

gray parrot
Psittacus erithacus

Conversing with the dolphins

Dolphins really seem to enjoy contact with humans, while humans have always been fascinated and enchanted by these aquatic mammals. Their outstanding memory as well as their ability to imitate and learn make dolphins one of the most intelligent animals on the planet. Time and time again, humans have attempted in vain to understand and decode their language. In Hawaii, trainers invented a language of sounds and signals using their hands and arms, which they were able to teach to dolphins.

bottle-nosed dolphin
Tursiops trunctatus

A lucrative partnership

Some African communities enjoy wild bee honey thanks to the help of a bird, the greater indicator. Humans ask the birds to guide them to the honey by whistling into their clenched fists. Greater indicators, who know where the nests are located, fulfil their companions' request, leading them in the right direction by crying out persistently along the way. When they reach their destination, humans gather the precious honey and give the birds a well-deserved portion of the loot.

greater indicator
Indicator indicator

Are you curious?

The pigeon navigates by observing the position of the sun, the moon and the stars, and by registering the location of mountains and rivers along its route as well as the earth's magnetic field over the course of its journey.

These ones are usurpers
of communication

Many animals borrow the voices, attitudes, gestures and sometimes even the coloring of the animals around them. Sly and skilled, these usurpers always get what they want! Disguised in the same orange and black colors as monarch butterflies with poisonous flesh, viceroy butterflies trick their adversaries by pretending they have the same nasty taste as their doubles. Small caterpillars are extremely talented actors, writhing their upper bodies like deadly poisonous snakes and… Discover the tricks of these pirates of communication.

Masked fish

Adorned with bright colors, threadfin butterfly fish wear a unique disguise that really throws their predators for a loop. At the front of their bodies, their eyes are hidden by a black mask, while at the rear, near the caudal fin, they sport a small spot that looks like an eye… As predators swim toward what they believe to be the head of their prey, these little tricksters take off at full speed, leaving total confusion in their wake!

threadfin butterfly fish
Chaetodon auriga

A masterful impostor

Thick-billed euphonias imitate the song of the yellow-green vireo so well that they are mistaken for individuals of this species! When a predator approaches their nest, euphonias emit the vireo's cry of distress. Convinced that the alarm was sounded by one of their own, vireos rush at the intruder to chase it away. Meanwhile, comfortably hidden among the leaves, euphonias benefit from the vireos' protection without having to lift a feather to defend themselves!

yellow-green vireo
Vireo flavoviridis

thick-billed euphonia
Euphonia laniirostris

jumping spider
Salticus scenicus

When flies act like spiders...

What better way to avoid being devoured than to speak the same language as your enemy? Sporting intricate patterns, fruit flies can venture close to the formidable jumping spider, without fear of being devoured… As the enemy approaches, these flies flick their wings from side to side, imitating the movement of a jumping spider's legs. Tricked into thinking the fly is a fellow spider, the spider doesn't attack, thus sparing the fly's life!

25

fruit fly
Rhagoletis zephyria

Are you curious?

Much sought-after by aquarists, butterfly fish can live for many years in captivity. Although they eat all kinds of food, they are delicate and do not reproduce in aquariums.

1. **Gray long-eared bat (p. 2)**
   (central Europe)

2. **Honeybee (p. 3)**
   (all over the world)

3. **Garden spider (p. 3)**
   (from Boston, Massachusetts to the Great Lakes; Canada, Québec, Europe)

4. **South American electric eel (p. 3)**
   (South America: Amazonia and Guyana)

5. **Nightingale (p. 4)**
   (northwest Africa, central and eastern Europe, western Asia)

6. **Right whale (p. 5)**
   (northern and southern Atlantic and Pacific oceans)

7. **European tree frog (p. 5)**
   (western, central and southern Europe [except the British Isles])

8. **Woodchuck (p. 5)**
   (North America)

9. **Palm cockatoo (p. 6)**
   (New Guinea, northeastern Australia, Aru Islands)

10. **Common furniture beetle (p. 7)**
    (Europe)

11. **Common flicker (p. 7)**
    (North America and Central America as far as Nicaragua)

12. **European rabbit (p. 7)**
    (Europe, northern Africa, introduced into Australia and southwestern South America)

13. **Eastern diamondback rattlesnake (p. 8)**
    (from southeastern North Carolina to eastern Louisiana and all of Florida)

14. **Bow-winged grasshopper (p. 9)**
    (Europe, Siberia, northern Africa)

15. **Gray gurnard (p. 9)**
    (Atlantic Ocean, from Norway to southern Africa, North Sea, Baltic Sea)

16. **Mole cricket (p. 9)**
    (Europe, western Asia, northern Africa)

17. **Red howler (p. 10)**
    (Colombia, Venezuela, Peru, Brazil, Guyana)

18. **Three-wattled bellbird (p. 11)**
    (South America, from Honduras to western Panama)

19. **Northern gannet (p. 11)**
    (east and west coasts of the North Atlantic)

20. **Red deer (p. 11)**
    (Europe, northern and central Asia, northern Africa, North America)

21. **Ruff (p. 12)**
    (Europe, Asia, Africa, Australia)

22. **Three-spined stickleback (p. 13)**
    (Europe, Siberia, East Asia)

23. **Palmated newt (p. 13)**
    (England, western Germany, Belgium, Netherlands, France, Switzerland, northern Spain)

A LANGUAGE FOR EVERY OCCASION...

To attract partners and for mating

Animals...	...and their language
Croaking gouramis (*Trichopsis vittata*)	Males emit sounds produced by exhaling air through their gills.
Black grouses (*Lyrurus tetrix*)	Males simulate combat with other males to attract females.
Sea horses (Syngnathidae family)	Males make dry clicking sounds produced by the friction of the cranial bones. The sound is amplified by the swim bladder.
Glowworms (Lophiidae family)	Males and females communicate using light codes produced through bioluminescence.
Sea urchins (Echinides order)	Males and females give off a scent to attract a mate.
Electric rays (Rajiformes order)	Males produce an electric field that signals their aggressiveness to other males.

To mark territory and protect it against intruders

Animals...	...and their language
Cicadas (Cicadidae family)	Males produce sounds using special muscles to vibrate membranes on either side of their abdomens.
Siamangs (*Symphalangus syndactylus*)	Males cry out by inflating the vocal pouch located below their throats.
Squirrels (Rajiformes order)	Some skin glands produce an odorous substance.
Antelopes (Bovidae family)	Glands under the eyes or between the horns produce an odorous substance.
Garibaldis (*Hypsypops rubicundus*)	These fish grind their upper and lower pharyngal teeth together to produce a sound that is amplified by the swim bladder.

To intimidate the enemy and send a clear warning

Animals...	...and their language
Gorillas (Pongidae family)	Males beat their chests with clenched fists.
Earwigs (Forficulidae family)	Males and females adopt an intimidating posture by raising their pincers up above their backs.
Dendrobates frogs (Ranidae family)	Their bright colors warn of their toxicity.
Swans (Anatidae family)	Males whistle as they spread their wings.
Owls (Strigidae family)	They puff up and spread their wings to appear bigger than they actually are.

To warn of danger

Animals...	...and their language
Vervet monkeys (*Cercopithecus aethiops*)	They use various cries, each of which warns of a specific danger.
Beavers (Castoridae family)	They use their tail to produce a slapping sound on the water's surface.
Earthworms (*Lumbricus terrestris*)	They secrete an odorous substance in the soil.

ANIMALS AND THEIR LANGUAGE

Mammals	bear	growl
	beaver	moan, tail-slap
	boar	chirrup, grunt, snort, squeak
	buffalo, ox	moo
	caribou, stag, deer, buck, wapiti	bark, bell, roar, scream, troat
	cat	meow, growl, purr
	dog	bark, growl, yelp
	donkey, mule, onager	bray
	elephant	trumpet
	fox	bark, howl, scream, whimper, yap
	hippopotamus	grunt
	hog	grunt, snort
	horse	neigh
	hyena	cackle, whoop, yell
	jaguar	growl, grunt, mew, snarl
	lamb, ewe, goat, kid, sheep	bleat
	leopard	rasp, roar
	lion	growl, roar, snarl
	moose	moo
	pig	grunt, snort
	porcupine	grunt, rattle, rustle
	rabbit	scream
	ram, camel, dromedary, llama	gargle, roar
	rhinoceros	honk, puff, roar, shriek, snort, squeal
	skunk	grunt, purr, whistle
	wolf	bark, growl, howl, whine, yip
	woodchuck	screech
Birds	barn owl	hiss, hoot, screech, shrill, snore
	cowbird	gurgle, whistle
	crow	caw
	cuckoo	cuckoo
	duck	quack
	eagle	cackle, squeal, trumpet, yelp
	grouse	cluck, whirr
	harrier	whistle
	hawfinch	pipe, trill, whistle
	lark	chime
	magpie	chatter
	owl	hoot, screech
	pigeon	coo
	ringdove or woodpigeon	coo, warble
	rooster	crow, sing
	sparrow	chirp
	swan	trumpet, whistle
	turkey	gobble
	warbler	trill, warble
	woodcock	trill, twang, warble
Reptiles and amphibians	crocodile	moan, wail
	snake	hiss
	toad, frog	croak
Insects	bee, bumblebee, wasp, fly	buzz, drone
	cicada, grasshopper, cricket	chirr, stridulate

For further information...

gray long-eared bat
Plecotus austriacus

size and weight	40 to 52 mm; 7 to 14 g
distribution	central Europe
habitat	forests, cultivated land, buildings
diet	insects
reproduction	1 offspring
life span	15 years

class Mammalia
order Chiroptera
family Vespertilionidae

nightingale
Luscinia megarhynchos

size and weight	16 to 16.5 cm long; 23 g on average
distribution	northwestern Africa, central and eastern Europe, western Asia
habitat	woodlands, bushes
diet	insects and other invertebrates, berries and fruit
reproduction	4 or 5 eggs per year; 14-day incubation period

class Birds
order Passeriformes
family Turdidae

palm cockatoo
Probosciger aterrimus

size	50 to 63 cm
distribution	New Guinea, northeastern Australia, Aru Islands
habitat	forests, savannahs, woodlands
diet	insect larvae, nuts, seeds, fruit, flower buds
reproduction	1 egg; 1-month incubation period
predators	Some lizards eat eggs
life span	30 years

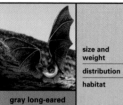

eastern diamondback rattlesnake
Crotalus adamanteus

size	84 to 183 cm; record length of 243.8 cm
distribution	from southeastern North Carolina to eastern Louisiana and all of Florida
habitat	forests, scrubland, near bodies of water
diet	eggs, birds, rodents
reproduction	viviparous, 10 to 12 offspring

class Reptiles
order Squamata
family Viperidae

30

red howler
Alouatta seniculus

size and weight	46 to 72 cm; tail: 50 to 75 cm; 4.5 to 8 kg
distribution	Colombia, Venezuela, Peru, Brazil and Guyana
habitat	tropical forests, savannahs, mixed forests
diet	leaves and fruit
reproduction	1 offspring; 186- to 194-day incubation period

class Mammalia
order Primata
family Cebidae

ruff
Philomachus pugnax

size and weight	20 to 32 cm; 110 to 245 g
distribution	Europe, Asia, Africa, Australia
habitat	tundras, marshlands, wetlands
diet	snails, worms, crustaceans, insects, freshwater algae, grains of rice and sorghum
reproduction	4 eggs; 20-day incubation period
life span	10 years

class Birds
order Charadriiformes
family Scolopacidae

blue peacock
Pavo cristatus

size	males: 2 to 2.3 m long (2/3 for the train); female: 86 cm
distribution	Sri Lanka, India, Pakistan
habitat	forests, semi-open terrain, near bodies of water
diet	seeds, fruit, insects, cobras and other reptiles, mammals
reproduction	3 to 5 eggs; 28-day incubation period
predators	tigers, leopards, humans

class Birds
order Galliformes
family Phasianidae

common chimpanzee
Pan troglodytes

size and weight	64 to 94 cm; 40 to 55 kg
distribution	western and central Africa, from Senegal to Burundi and in the Congo basin in Tanzania
habitat	wooded savannahs, rain forests
diet	fruit, leaves, flowers, buds, bark, seeds, insects
reproduction	1 baby; 230-day gestation period
predators	leopard
life span	50 years in captivity

class Mammalia
order Primata
family Pongidae

muskrat
Ondatra zibethicus

size	25 to 35 cm; tail: 20 to 25 cm
distribution	North America, introduced to Europe and Siberia
habitat	quiet rivers, ponds, marshlands
diet	aquatic and cultivated plants, sometimes aquatic molluscs
reproduction	1 to 3 offspring; 20- to 30-day gestation period
predators	foxes, racoons, raptors
life span	3 to 4 years

class Mammalia
order Rodentia
family Arvicolidae

Japanese macaque
Macaca fuscata

size and weight	54 to 72 cm, including the tail; 8 to 18 kg
distribution	Japan
habitat	dense forests, steep mountains
diet	berries, fruit, nuts, leaves, buds, insects, eggs, snails, mushrooms
reproduction	1 offspring; approximately 173-day gestation period
predators	lynx, coyotes
life span	over 30 years

class Mammalia
order Primata
family Cercopithecidae

feral pigeon
Columba livia

size	33 cm long
distribution	Europe, northern Africa, Asia, India
habitat	cities, open areas, rocky outcrops and cliffs
diet	seeds, snails and worms
reproduction	1 to 2 eggs; 17-day incubation period
predators	felines and other carnivores

class Birds
order Columbiformes
family Columbidae

threadfin butterfly fish
Chaetodon auriga

size	23 cm
distribution	warm regions of the Pacific, Atlantic and Indian oceans
habitat	coasts, sandy and coralline ocean floors
diet	crustaceans, worms, anemones and seaweed
predators	fish, humans
life span	several years, in captivity

class Fish
order Perciformes
family Chaetodontidae

Glossary

Adorn
Display something or wear it in such a way that it is clearly visible.

Aquarist
Person who keeps tropical fish in an aquarium.

Bacteria
Microscopic single-celled organisms.

Beam
All of the light rays originating from a single source (for example, a flashlight beam).

Bioluminescence
Production of a light signal by a living creature (for example a firefly).

Breastplate
Area covering the breast.

Caruncle
A fleshy red outgrowth on the head and throat of certain birds, like roosters.

Caudal
Relating to the tail.

Chivalry
The qualities of an ideal knight or warrior.

Cohesion
Bond or force uniting the members of a group.

Colony
A group of animals that live together. This word is often used to refer to a group of birds that gather together to reproduce.

Crescendo
A gradual increase in the volume of sound.

Defecate
To discharge feces; to move bowels.

Diurnal
Occurring in the daytime.

Electroplaque
A group of cells found in some fish that carries an electric charge.

Elytron
The hard, horny forewing of beetles, and of some other insects, that is not used to fly but to protect the hind wing.

Expose
To display or make visible.

Gill
An organ of aquatic animals such as fish, located on the side of the head, that enables them to breathe.

Grooming
The act of removing lice one at a time from another living being.

Hammer
To hit again and again.

Larynx
An organ that permits the production of sound and is located in the upper part of the neck, above the pharynx (see this word).

Mock
Not real; designed to trick someone.

Nibble
To eat away with quick, small bites, as a rabbit or a mouse does.

Olfaction
Sense of smell.

Parasite
An organism that lives on, with or in another, from which it gets its food.

Percussionist
Musician who plays an instrument that requires striking to produce a rhythm, such as a drum or cymbal.

Pharyngal
Relating to the pharynx.

Pharynx
Canal between the mouth and the esophagus containing the respiratory and digestive routes.

Pheromones
Secretion produced by animals that trigger specific behavior in a fellow member of the species.

Putrid
Describes an extremely unpleasant odor and that can cause nausea.

Ritual
Rules, gestures and actions that recur regularly or are repeated more or less the same way.

Salivary gland
Organ that excretes a thickish liquid known as saliva.

Stridulation
A shrill shrieking noise produced by certain insects, including cicadas and grasshoppers, by rubbing striated organs together.

Subordinated
Occupying a lower rank in the social organization.

Swim bladder
Among certain fish, an internal sac that fills with gas, enabling the animal to float in water.

Thorax
Among insects, the division just behind the head and neck, to which is attached the wings and legs.

Toxicity
Characteristic of a substance harmful to a living creature and that acts as a poison.

Trill
Sound produced by the rapid and prolonged repetition of two notes a scale degree apart.

Ultrasound
Sound that the human ear cannot perceive because the frequency is too high.

Usurper
Individual who uses, without right, an item or function belonging to another individual.

Voltage
The strength of electric pressure in an electric current.

Index

The terms in **bold characters** refer to an illustration; those in *italics* indicate a keyword.

So Many Ways to Communicate was created and produced by **QA International**, a division of Les Éditions Québec Amérique inc, 329, rue de la Commune Ouest, 3ᵉ étage, Montréal (Québec) H2Y 2E1 Canada **T** 514.499.3000 **F** 514.499.3010
©1999 Éditions Québec Amérique inc.

ISBN 2-89037-982-5

Printed and bound in Canada

10 9 8 7 6 5 4 3 2 1 99